Homosexuality :
The Word
vs
Religious Tradition

J. Karl Jackson
David Oestrick

Homosexuality: The Word vs. Religious Tradition

Copyright © 2016, 2020 by
J. Karl Jackson & David Oestrick.
All rights reserved

Self published by,
J. Karl Jackson & David Oestrick
Sand Point, Michigan 48755

First Edition/Second Printing (with corrections) 2020
ISBN 978-1-54392-960-7

Unless otherwise indicated all scripture quotations are
taken from the *King James Version of the Bible*

Contents

INTRODUCTION

For years now, many religious organizations have pitted themselves against the gay community. In some cases they've almost become the gay community's worst enemy. What's interesting is that, back in bible days, according to scripture, religious organizations were once the biggest enemy of Jesus as well. Within the stories of how Jesus victored over his enemies, there is a lot the gay community can learn in how to face the religious organizations of our day. In this book "Homosexuality: The Word versus Religious Tradition" we attempt to lay out *a very thorough study of scripture* that may help bring some victories to pass for those who face those challenges. To the very least, we trust from reading it that some will find peace with God.

The Sadducees and the Pharisees, two of the most reputable religious organizations in the community of Jesus' time, found themselves over and over again in a *spirit* that continually worked to sabotage the ministry of Jesus. That same deceptive spirit is still well and very much alive today and it is known in our time throughout the Body of Christ as the *"Religious Spirit"*. This *spirit* inspires its subjects to use scripture to belittle in the same way that Satan did and mimics religious sounding phrases ultimately found nowhere supported in the Word. Today, *this spirit* has found high positions in some of the most well known religious organizations of our time. In most recent years it has been found focusing much of its attention on those who are LGBT.

This spirit is by no means a new enemy.   Its leader is the same enemy   Jesus   faced   in   Matthew 4 : 1-11.   He defeated it victoriously by saying "It is written"!! and then responding to him with the Word of God. This book, "Homosexuality: The Word versus Religious Tradition" was written to assist believers in their battles with this spirit. WE shed light on how this vicious *religious spirit* has manifested itself in our history. It also shows how to use the Word of God to defeat it in its battle against those who are LGBT. According to II Corinthians 2:14, it's a battle in which believers shall be triumphant.

Jesus warned us of the look this spirit sports, calling those who submitted to this *"religious spirit"* hypocrites. He said,

Matthew 6:5
5 they love to pray standing in the synagogues and on the corners of the streets that they might be seen of men...and ...

Matthew 6:16
16 ...disfigure their faces to show men that they are fasting

Not only did he not endorse much of their actions, he almost never favored any of the religious organizations that they associated with either. He never sided with them *against* the community the way that many religious organizations band together and go against communities today. He never rallied against gays the way so many religious organizations do today. In fact, while people today would have you think that He did, Jesus never spoke one thing in the scripture against gays, period. Gays were never the enemy in the way that religious organizations have placed them today. What you will find in scripture, rather than of Jesus speaking against gays, is Jesus railing and railing against the religious organizations of His day. The two He railed against the most were the most reputable religious organizations in all Jerusalem.

One religious organization, "The Sadducees", came to be known for honoring "The Torah". It is a writing that, at that time, was said to include only those commands that Hebrews believed God, himself had given. The other organization, the Pharisee's honored what was called "The Oral Torah" which was said to contain not only the things God commanded but the things that Moses, himself, commanded as well.

Both of these two groups were very highly esteemed organizations. Both were known throughout all Jerusalem. The *spirit* in which both worked had brought them to such high places, which they were ultimately viewed by many as the very spokesmen of God. They were also looked upon as experts of the scripture in the same way we look at the leaders of large religious groups in our day. Because of their expertise, they were also looked upon as Judges of the community and determined for them what was righteous and what was not. In fact, the standards for righteousness that they laid out and taught were set so high that even Jesus himself said " except your righteousness shall exceed the righteousness of the scribes and Pharisees you shall in no case enter the kingdom of heaven (Matt 5:20). Their standards were exceptionally high but still not high enough to enter the kingdom as it was righteousness on the outside that had never reached their insides. Jesus said …

Matt 23: 27

27 *"you are like unto whitewashed sepulchers which indeed appear beautiful outwards but are within full of dead bones and uncleanness"*

Jesus almost never had good words for the Sadducees and the Pharisees who operated in this „religious spirit". It seemed to be their mission in life to always hound those who would not honor their religious traditions. They hounded them the same way the religious organizations of our day came against those who refused to honor the idea of traditional marriage. Just like they wanted the government to enforce traditional marriage, the Sadducees and Pharisees worked with their officials to enforce their traditions on people as well . And then, finally, these religious groups were able to legally plot the murder of Jesus and do it successfully. They did all of this proudly and with honor in the names of the religious organizations they embraced. It was THAT *"religious spirit"* that John the Baptist saw and called out, saying...

Matthew 23:33

33 *"You generation of vipers!! Who has warned YOU, to flee from the wrath to come? "*

Having seen the religious operate in this spirit and abuse this power for years, John was saying "Why would anybody tell you, you can escape the wrath to come? " From that time on, he and Jesus never backed away from an opportunity to *call out those operating in this "religious spirit"*. And in same spirit of Jesus, John, and the prophets of old who always raised their voices calling this spirit out, defenders of the faith today should be just as vocal against this *"religious spirit"* which is now targeting itself against those who are LGBT.

Isaiah 58:1
1 "Cry aloud, spare not, lift up thy voice like a trumpet and show MY people their transgression and the house of Jacob their sin

Note : Almost every time you hear the prophets of old cry like this, it always refers to HIS PEOPLE , he wants HIS people to see their errors and not those of the world who don't know Him.

"Homosexuality: The Word versus Religious Tradition" is written to equip believers to stand up to the people of God who have submitted themselves to the spirit of the Sadducee. It is the same spirit that has been called by many today , *"the religious spirit'*. He is one *sent by Satan to deceive* by inspiring its subjects to use scripture to belittle, in the same way that Satan did. He mimics religious sounding phrases ultimately found to be nowhere supported in the Word.

In the bible, the Apostle Paul ran across a woman with a similar spirit . Scripture says she had a spirit of divination. The greek (in Strongs #4436) says it was a *"spirit of a python"*. A spirit *sent to deceive* as a snake in the same way a person operating in a „religious spirit" deceives. It is also the same spirit we read earlier that John the Baptist had called out.

Acts 16: 17 The same followed Paul and us crying, These men are servants of the most high God which show us the way of salvation.

Her deception was to make herself *sound as if she was a supporter of the Apostles and the gospel which they preached.* Paul, however, recognizing who *really* sent her, found himself instead grieved and thus commanded that this *deceptive religious spirit* come out of her and the devil came out.

He later warns us of people like this and says that they ...

2 Timothy 3:5
5 "Having a form of godliness but they deny the power thereof. From such stay away"

The deception that the person working in this demonic "religious spirit" comes with, makes the person that it's working with appear to be coming in love as a dedicated servant of God. But, in truth, it is only really there to ultimately condemn. It is always when one doesn't recognize this spirit that he finds himself a victim of his deceit.

Generally, when a "religious spirit" is at work in someone, the person it's operating through will speak out some popular religious phrase often repeated by Christians. It almost always evokes the word "God "or the "Bible" to overly promote and give itself scriptural authority, when in actuality, the phrase has no real support from the Bible at all.

One operating in a "religious spirit" that's sent to oppress those who are LGBT can very easily be spotted. One of that spirit's most famous phrases is...,

"The bible says homosexuality is a sin".

When using the phrase "the bible says", the phrase commands the attention of the believer. It is when the phrase is completed with "homosexuality is a sin" that the deception begins. The phrase is found nowhere at all in the bible as the person has claimed it is.

While the statement made may sound very innocent , as the spirit behind it intended it, it is actually one that's very vicious. This statement has run people away from God and His church into oppressive relationships and many, because of it, have even ended their lives in suicide. The proof that such a statement is engineered by Satan and not by God, is that it often drives many to death. Jesus said that it is ...

John 10:10
10 The enemy comes only to steal, kill and destroy, I have come that they might have life and have it more abundantly

Anything less than a full abundant life filled with joy is not a life that God has planned for any. It is our plan in writing this book that many will begin to stand up against this "religious spirit" that manifests itself for the destruction of innocent lives. It is our hope that we can also bring people to the path of the kind of life that Jesus ordained for all to live according his word. This book is also written so that readers will learn ALL the deceptive "religious phrases" and "bible misquotes" that those who operate in the "religious spirit" use. This book will also compare each of these common religious phrases used to what was actually written in the Word. This will ultimately also help readers to share these truths with those they meet, those who have "ears to hear".

Another statement that the "religious spirit" will use to intimidate those whose attention it captures, is saying that
"homosexuality is written about all throughout the bible".

Here, once again, the listener is told something that is a total untruth. It is being used to intimidate its listener into another a huge deception. Not only is the statement untrue but the word "homosexual" is found nowhere at all in any of the original biblical writings introduced to the world thousands of years ago.

It has only been in this last century that some publishers of the newer versions have even begun to add the word "homosexual" into the scripture. This is why reading newer versions are not always advised for thorough studies. Often, the newer the version, the further away we get from what was originally written. In "Homosexuality: The Word versus Religious Tradition", the authors will show what was written in several of the original manuscripts in order to bear out what the biblical writers originally wrote regarding some of these scriptures.

To support the claim that "homosexuality is written about all throughout the bible", a person operating in "the religious spirit" will begin to quote several scriptural references typically spoken out so that they can support their claim. The believer who doesn't know that the persons statement is not true, generally begins to feel lost when these verses are quoted. Once again, he finds him or herself intimidated which is a mild form of fear. This, once again, evokes a spirit that the word clearly affirms, is not a spirit of God.

2 Timothy 1:7 ..
7 "God has not given us the spirit of fear"

Those who have read this book will, however, learn that out of all the 31,102 verses in bible, "the religious spirit" will only find himself referencing seven (7). Even in quoting the 7 that they do, the number in no way substantiates the phrase they use when saying "all throughout the bible". It's another statement again used to intimidate.

Then the "religious spirit" will show the 7 scriptures they've referenced and explain that they mean things the reader himself won't even see. Not, that is, until the person quoting it has given his false explanation.

Once the spirit's target has seen the scripture and heard the explanations (when he is not bible literate) and *even though he doesn't understand* , he will generally just accept it. It's when this tactic is used by the *religious spirit* that many come to believe that "the bible is hard to understand". This is another untruth as scripture says ...

Psalms 119:130
130 "The entrance of His Word gives light: it gives understanding to the simple."

Today, because of this religious spirit, there are many who won't even read the bible saying its too confusing which shows it successes. Yet the Word says ….

I Corinthians 14:33
33 "God is not the author of confusion but of peace".

The witch hunts, condemnations and protest against gays we see today are things you will never read about in the bible. They didn't have them because in those days they had a different understanding of those scriptures. The aim of this book is to show that the understanding that they had during bible days of these 7 scriptures were not the same understandings that the "religious spirit" pushes on LGBT"s today. After reading this book, readers won't ever again be confronted with anything quoted from the bible on the subject that he hasn't learned to understand in its proper meaning.

<u>Below we have listed the 7 scriptures spouted</u>

Gen 19.
Which talks about Sodom. We talk about the Hebrew word "yada" also, who the Word really says Sodomites wer

Jude 7,
in the new testament, which said they went after "strange flesh",. We talk about its greek word , "heteros"

Leviticus 18 :22.
talks about men lying with men. Seeing it in its full context you see to whom it refers and

Rom 1:26
the one scripture referring to women doing things unnatural which has a very different meaning in its original context

I Cor 6:9 *Talks about the effeminate. We will show it in its original translation before it was changed.*

I Tim 1:10
talks about "men who abuse themselves with mankind" We show this as it was originally written.

II Tim 3:2-3
Is about the men becoming "lovers of themselves". We share how this has been terribly misinterpreted.

Each of these scriptures *the religious spirit* refers to has to be understood as they were written in their original languages and context. Generally, if you ask the "religious spirit" who quotes them, if they done such a study, they will undoubtedly answer "no". Not even some of the world greatest religious leaders have studied these out because they have no personal interest in referencing them other than to condemn. Those who have been afflicted, however, by this spirit would benefit from such a study. That is why we wrote the book.

It also should be noted that "Homosexuality: The Word versus Religious Tradition" is not an interpretation that we ourselves have personally developed regarding these scriptures. In fact ours is not an interpretation at all. It is *a focus on translation* that anybody will be able to come to on their own with the same tools used by the nation's top bible scholars. [An interpretation is how someone *sees* a scripture and everybody can see them differently. A translation, translates it back to its original languages. If done right, then most will end up with the same things.] Most interpret, this books translates.

All of the translations in this book can be confirmed via the Strong concordance, Young's concordance, Vine's Expository of the Bible, any Hebrew, Aramaic or Greek Lexicon. It should also be noted that any bible reference or version we quote can be picked up at any public book or bible store. If needed, they can also be confirmed by the Blue-letter Bible source found online.

These are all legitimate sources. All of which have been referenced by the nation's top bible scholars. Some are over 100s of years old. We merely share what these references are and allow our readers to view these scriptures as they are written in their original languages and contexts. In the process, readers will also find themselves even learning a little Hebrew and some Greek. It is also our hope that these studies will prompt our readers to begin to expand their library of study aides. This will ultimately inspire readers to become better students of the Word not only on the subject of "homosexuality" but any topic they're confronted with.

A good student of the Word should always know that the truths scriptures reveal will never be fully understood by anyone from mere reading or by shear meditation. It must be closely studied in its original languages and its verses in their full contexts, for its greatest revelations.

Just one more note before closing this intro. It should come as no surprise to any believer that his greatest enemy would be leaders of the community's religious organizations. It was this same "religious spirit" Jesus was faced with regularly and, when He did, He minced no words .

Here he said to them ……

Matthew 23:13
***13** "Woe unto you, you scribes and Pharisees, hypocrites! For you shut up the kingdom of heaven against men: for you neither go in yourselves, neither do you allow them who are entering to go in".*

He never had a lot of good things to say about these people and when they come against you, He understands the same challenge. He had to constantly face this "religious spirit " Himself . So he understands. God is on YOUR side. The Word is on your side. The apostles are on your side and we are on your side, too. Hear the words of the Apostle Paul

Romans 8:31
***31** "What, then, shall we say in response to these things? If God is for us, who can be against us*

It is our prayer that reading "Homosexuality: The Word versus Religious Tradition", will help our readers sense the presence of God near.

CHAPTER ONE

The Original Written Word OR is it *Just Religious Tradition?*

"The Word" that We Hear Preached Today

More than ever before today, more believers are coming out to claim the inheritance God has promised to them with the saints (Ephesians 1:11) In 1969, after the Stonewall uprising, many of those coming out to claim this inheritance were believers who also began to identify themselves as LGBT. Much of this bold freedom is due to a discovery that a lot of what religious tradition has taught on the subject of homosexuality (and SO many other things) has not been found supported by anything God ever said or inspired in *the original written Word* . Many of these discoveries have brought radical changes into the lives of believers and brought them into a closer relationship with Jesus and many into a much deeper appreciation of His Word.

It is through the testimonies left recorded in the *original written Word* that many believers today have come to understand the God of all creation and his Son the Lord Jesus Christ . It is also through the *original inspired Word,* that many testify to having found personal salvation and ultimate liberation. It is not been the same testimony, however, with those who have "gotten religion" and merely taken on what men have passed down through religious tradition. For some, it has brought no change to their hearts at all. They have just gained a religion with traditions that have left them in churches for eons in darkness with unanswered questions about a God and his ways. Many of them teach that, He is a God who "has *mysterious* ways and plans that no one can understand". Yet, in the original written Word it says, " He has ...

Ephesians 1:9
9....made known unto us the mystery of His will according to His good pleasure which He has purposed in Himself

The View or Religious Traditionalist

Religious Traditionalists teach we can't know God's will. The Word teaches He's made known to us His will. Religious tradition has taught us that we are sinners when the word calls us saints (I Corinthians 1:2, Philippians 1:2) It has taught us that only God has power ,when the Word teaches us that WE have power (Luke 10:19). It's taught that gay believers are going to hell when the Word says that gay believers, like all believers, have eternal life (John 3:16). While religious tradition claims to uphold the bible, it almost always has been found throughout history to teach what is polar opposite of the Word. Jesus made attempts to make the religious organizations of his day aware of this. He said to them, "You are ...

Mark 7:13
13 ....making the Word of God on none effect through your tradition which you have delivered.

In the same way Jesus condemned religious tradition of his day for rendering God's Word ineffective, it is time for us to take that same position today against those using the Word incorrectly against gays.

Understanding that both are often found in conflict should give us all a fervor to look at the scripture and more particularly those verses quoted against homosexuality. It is also only in studying it that we will find the words God himself inspired on the subject and it is only in *closely looking* at it that we will learn what's just religious tradition and what God himself inspired in the *original written Word* .

II Timothy 3:16
16 All scripture is given by divine inspiration of God, and is profitable for doctrine

Hundreds and hundreds of years of work has gone into preserving what we hail today as the Word of God. However, while much has been done over thousands of years to keep this wonderful treasure, keeping it to perfection has not been done *by its experts* without infallibility. Therefore, those who seek its true "truths", are challenged to do much more than just read them for enjoyment and devotional meditations. This is particularly true of those who wish to learn what was written in it about homosexuality, if there was ever anything written in it on the subject at all. There are many deep truths to be discovered by believers who are willing to do more than just read and are willing to trust the Spirit within and study to seek them out.They are not writings just to be read as a regular book or even a newspaper.The Apostle Paul, one of its authors, says..

II Timothy 2:15
15 Study to show thyself approved unto God, (but as) a workman that needeth not to be ashamed ,rightly dividing the word of truth.

Hebrews 11:6
6 He is a rewarder of them that diligently seek him

I John 2:27
27 But the anointing which ye have received, abideth IN YOU, and ye need not that any man teach you.

So, in studying out the subject of homosexuality to get a good understanding of what was recorded in the original written Word, it's very important that all the above be taken into account.

It should also be taken into account, while entering into this study, that you will find *many things that are in the original writings* that don't jibe with religious tradition. But don't be alarmed. Remember we read that Jesus said earlier in Mark 7:13, that religious traditions make the Word of non-effect.

So prepare yourself in tackling the subject on homosexuality as if you are entering into a spiritual warfare the same as did Jesus. This is the war of *"The Original Written Word versus Religious Tradition."*

Quoting "Versions" Vs The Original Written Word

Today when most people, who are staunched deeply in their religious traditions, speak about homosexuality, they generally reference different quotes from the bible and say, "This is not me just talking this is what God says about it.

In as much confidence and authority as they speak, most don't even realize that what they are reading and quoting is *NOT what God said at all* but only someone giving their "version" of what God said . This can very easily be confirmed as right on the front cover of almost every bible that any one may hold, you will see the word "version".

It is only on a very rare occasion that someone quotes from what was originally written and you will almost never hear someone who's staunched in religious tradition quote from it. Many of them speaking don't even know that there is anything more original than what they read from. Truth is, even if they read what was originally written on the subject of homosexuality, most would reject it since what was originally written in it wouldn't jibe with tradition. Nor does anything in the original writing condemn those who are gay . What you will find from reading this book is that there are things in the newer "versions", however, that DO condemn.

In this first chapter we will look at one of the verses used today to condemn gays as it was written in some of the earliest "versions" of scripture. We will compare it to what is now written in the newer versions. It is our hope in doing these comparisons that readers would be encouraged to do more than just read but to study the scripture. Every subject found in the Word is worthy of this kind of intense study. The revelations you will find from thorough study will be amazing !!

Things would be a lot different for those who are LGBT if today we still had what was originally recorded and not just what was left for us in the hundreds of different versions of scripture generally quoted and referred to today. Surely they would be referred to by many a whole lot more. Unfortunately, however, none of the original writing written by Old and New Testament writers were saved. Every last one of the original recordings have been lost.

While no one today has been able to recover any of the actual original recordings, what we have been blessed to find are the early manuscripts and many of their earliest versions. It is in these very early ancient writings (that were produced before any of the versions most read today) that we will find how the 7 scriptures quoted today against gays were originally written.

The Original Manuscripts

The "Manuscripts" we have today are no more than *handwritten copies of copies* of what was originally written, as the printing press hadn't been invented yet in these times. While we do, however, have some of these ancient copies, no one even knows the names of the scribes who wrote them or how close they are to what the original authors wrote.

Another important thing to note about the ancient manuscripts now held is that none of them were written in English as the English language did not yet exist. It wasn't until hundreds and hundreds of years after England was established as a nation and much later America, that the original Hebrew, Aramaic and Greek copies were finally translated to the English language.

In this book we will look at these very early language translations to see the 7 references that religious organizations typically quote on homosexuality. What you will find as we look at these scriptures is that in many cases, how the scripture originally read and what the versions look like today, is totally different.

As we begin to study these passages always keep in mind that the truths scripture reveal will never be fully understood by any from mere reading or by shear meditation. It must be closely studied in its original languages and its verses in their full contexts for its greatest revelations.

The View According to the Original English Version

The very first bible with The New Testament that was translated from the Greek to English was done by William Tyndale. It wasn't done until almost 1500 years after Christ. In looking at this very first work we will look at one of the 7 scriptures used today against gays. We will see how this scripture earliest appeared when first translated in English and then at the versions that came after it. Then, finally, we will see how the scripture looks now and how, in religious tradition, it is interpreted today.

The first scripture we will look at is II Timothy 2:1-3. When you read it you will find there is nothing in it that it suggests , even a little, that it refers to gays. Lets read.

II Timothy 3: 1-3 Tyndale 1534
(First English Translation ever)
1) This understand, that in the last days shall come perilous times.

2) For men shall be lovers of their own selves , covetous, boasters, proud , cursed speakers , disobedient to father and mother , unthankful, unholy
*3) **Unkind**, trucebreakers, stubborn, false accusers...*

There is one verse of these 3 scriptures that is sometimes quoted in reference to homosexuality but it's really out of sheer ignorance and that is verse 2 which says "men shall be lovers of their own selves". It is quoted by many as if it's saying, "in the last days… you will see men making love to men". But it's very clear to most that the writer is referring to men or mankind in general (women included) becoming more egotistical. There is nothing in that verse at all that even suggests homosexual activity but many in their attempts to condemn those who are gay, however, say that it does.

It is not that section of the verse, however, that's used most against gays today . It is something listed in verse 3, where it says "Unkind, trucebreakers, stubborn and false accusers ". The section of the verse that's used against gays today is the very first word in the verse which when it originally appeared in English, was translated as the word "unkind".

Again, anyone who would think this first word in verse 3 refers specifically to those who are LGBT would have to be ignorant. Surely everyone knows there are many more people in the world to whom this could apply, far outside of those in the gay community.

To see how this first word in verse 3 has been made to apply to gays today, 500 years later , it's important that we see the changes that occurred in this verse down through the years.

Many English versions of scripture were translated after William Tyndale first did his. One that was very popular was written twenty three years later. It is the version known as the Geneva Bible. Let's look at how they translated this scripture that today is so famously quoted against gays

II Timothy 3:1-3 Geneva Bible *1557*
(23 years after Tyndale)
1) This understand, that in the last days shall come
perilous times. 2)For men shall be lovers of their own selves ,
covetous, boasters, proud , cursed speakers , disobedient to
*father and mother , unthankful ,unholy 3)**Without charity,***
trucebreakers, stubborn, false accusers ...

What you should notice from this writing is that the Geneva Bible is almost an exact copy of the work Tyndale did 23 years earlier. This is good because the more closely the writings stay to the original, the better understanding we have of what was originally written. Remember Tyndale was the first to copy directly from the early Greek manuscripts.

Also note that while the Geneva Bible translators did translate *most* of the words Tyndale translated, word for word, they still did not copy *every word* the same. One word they did not translate the same was the first word found in verse 3. This is the same word that I mentioned earlier that today is often applied to gays.

When this word first appeared in the first English translations, it only appeared as one word, "Unkind" .The Geneva Bible translators not only changed the one word but added another word to it, making the one word that was there, now into two. Now, instead of just the word "Unkind" there, the Geneva Bible uses the two words, "Without charity".

Some may say, "Well …that is a difference, but is not a huge difference between someone who is "unkind" to someone who is "without charity", and I would agree, somewhat.

What should be noted, however, is not so much that the Geneva uses different words. What should be rather noted is that they *took the liberty, at their own authorization, to change* what was originally written. Can you imagine what the response would be today if a group of biblical scholars who supporters LGBT issues did such a change? Yet this group of scholars did and the work was still esteemed as the Word of God for all, even with all of its changes.

Even with this change, however, there was nothing in the words "without charity" that resembled same gender sexual activity at all. The next change to II Tim 3:2 was even more radical.

The next change appeared 52 years after the first Greek translation Tyndale made to English. This English version was produced by a group of priests in France that became known as the Rheims version. Let's look at how they translated the verse of our focus.

***II Timothy 3:1-3 Rheims Bible** 1582*
(52 years after Tyndale)
*1) And this know thou, that in the last days shall approach perilous times. 2) For men shall be lovers of their own selves , covetous, <u>haughty</u> , proud , <u>blasphemous</u>, not obedient <u>to parents</u>, unthankful , <u>wicked</u> 3)**without affection**, without peace, accusers, incontinent*

If you look at the words listed in VERSE 2 of the Rheims version you will note that now 4 of the 8 words listed in verse 2 were changed. (Incidentally, this group also added 14 more entire BOOKS that they found to this bible. Yet, none of these books are included in the majority of bibles sold today.)

Also note that in the Rheims version, there are yet *more new* words used in verse 3, the verse of our focus . 52 years prior, the first word was "unkind". 23 years after that, those words were changed to "without charity". In Rheims version 25 years later, it appears as the words "without affection". A very odd choice, considering that the first word "unkind", was VERY clear. Even a 5 year old today would understand what the word "unkind" would mean. The words "without charity" might be a little bit harder to understand at that age but an older child of 12 may be able to. The words "without affection", however, now are beginning to sound like a words that would require more thought or maybe even research. Why, though?

Who doesn't have "affections" for something? And how do you get the words "without affections" from the words "unkind "? And what was wrong with the word "unkind" that was there originally in the first place? It's a word that everybody understands. And how do any of these words translate into something that today is a scripture used against gays. In the next popular version you will see how the first word in verse 3 changed even more into words in the bible that are now used to condemn gays.

One of the next most popular bibles to come out to be well favored by the people of the 17th Century is still favored today and probably the most popular bible of all time . That bible is the Authorized King James Version, which came 29 years after The Rheims Version. Lets see how its version translated the verses of focus.

II Timothy 3:1-3 Authorized King James Bible *1611*
(87 years after Tyndale)
1)And this know also, that in the last days perilous times shall come.
2)For men shall be lovers of their own selves , covetous, boasters, proud , blasphemous, disobedient to parents, unthankful , unholy
*3)**Without NATURAL affection**, without peace, accusers, incontinent*

At this point, it probably becomes clear how the scripture we've been looking at is now used against LGBTs. It is assumed by many that the inter-actions heterosexuals have with their opposites is a *natural* process and that the interactions of those labeled homosexuals are not. That assumption made, according to that train of thought, makes gay people "without natural affections". That thinking, then in turn, makes them the horrid folks talked about in the letter to Timothy where its says, "in the last days perilous times shall come".

Before we talk about what's natural, however, and what's not natural, let's first talk about why the word "natural" is even appearing in this scripture at all. It is a word that was never there in the earliest writings. If it wasn't in the original writings, then it is a word NOT inspired by God . And if this particular word was never inspired by God, then how is it that so many religious leaders all over the world are so quick to use this scripture to say God condemns gays. What they have done is used words, that through careful study, anybody can learn *were never there in the original*.

A word written in the bible went from being the word "unkind" to 3 words that now read "without natural affections". We could do some research to trace back to see what the King James version meant by the phrase but it wouldn't give us the true meaning of what was originally written, as NONE OF THE WORDS in this verse the KJV"'s used for this word WERE EVEN THERE .

What we CAN do is, see what the word was that was used when this verse was originally written in the Greek. In this case, the original Greek word used was the word "Astergo", which Tyndale its original translator, 87 years before King James, defined as "one unkind, unloving *as one unloving unto his family or his nation*" .(which we will cover in more detail in another chapter).

So, using the original translator's word and definition, we can see there is nothing there in it at all that suggests that the words may be "without natural affection ". The word "unkind" looks nothing like the word "unnatural" and there was definitely nothing in the word "unkind" that suggests anything about sex or sexual preference. Therefore, this is a scripture that should never be applied in any way to those who are lesbian or gay.

What the Words Meant Then and What they Mean Now

In order to get an understanding and true meaning of any word in the bible you must know *not* what its definition is *today,* but what its definition was *at the time it was written*. Therefore, looking at a Webster's Dictionary for a word in the bible is never a good source to look at what the bible authors are saying . Why? Because Webster's give the definition to what *English* words mean .The bible, however, was originally written in Hebrew, Aramaic and Greek. To understand what the scripture truly means you must know what the words *were* then and what those words *meant* then. It is the only way you will really know the messages the bible's authors were working to convey. A Webster's dictionary will not give you those definitions. (A Hebrew and Greek Lexicon and Young's or Strong's Exhaustive Concordance will help with some of that).

Also you must remember, Webster's Dictionary was only written in the last 200 years and gives definitions of what the words meant when *he* wrote. The bible on the other hand was written thousands of years before him. So to get its original understandings you have to know what those definition meant then and not what they mean today. Words *and definitions continually change* throughout history.

Before I close out this chapter, I'd like to give you just an example of why it's important to do thorough studies when studying the scriptures using the kinds of aids just mentioned. This should be done, not only with scriptures that are used against those that who are lesbian and gay but on anything you need to know about the bible. Without this kind of study, it'd be hard for anyone to discover the many ancient deep truths it holds.

One example is found here ..

I Corinthians 14:34
34 .. Let your women keep silence in the church

Many religious organizations teach that this verse means women are to keep "silent" in the church and they use it to support that women should not preach. However, it does not say "let your women keep SILENT in the church. It says let your woman keep "SILENCE" in the church. In other words ,keep things quieted in the church. Actually , its original Greek is the word "siago" which means "to keep the peace", to keep things peaceful, to bring peace.

Pastor Selma, the pastor of the church that I attend in Detroit, has a dynamic ministry and, more in particular, is great at helping those who are LGBT find their "peace" with God (not to mention she has one of the most soothing voices I've ever heard). Definitely, she has chosen to answer the call in I Corinthian 14:34 and is surely one who fulfills the true meaning of this scripture. She brings peace to many spirits throughout the Body of Christ. It's a definition one would never get regarding this scripture verse from just reading it or meditating on it or just listening to some religious organizations teachings on it. It's a definition one would find only in "thorough study".

Many religious organizations today have leaders who are unlearned and unstudied who teach that the bible says "homosexuality is sin" . Yet the word "homosexual" is found nowhere in the *original* scripture at all. While it's not found anywhere in any of the original written writings, the word IS found in many of the later versions today. In doing thorough studies of the scripture, as we have done, with II Timothy 3:1-3, readers will learn what is just being passed down by religious tradition and what was actually given in the original written word.

Because of poor studies and just repeating what has been passed down through religious tradition , many religious organizations have brought total chaos to their communities regarding this subject. Many who are LGBT have been thrown into confusion as a result of this. This is a trick of Satan. However, the word says ...

II Corinthians 2:11
11 ...for we are not ignorant of his devices .

It is our goal by this book to encourage thorough study, as we have mentioned, so that believers will discover those treasures that are in the original written words and revealed in themselves.

CHAPTER TWO

Sodom, Gomorrah, The Sodomites and Sodomy

A Study of Genesis 19 and Jude 7

Among the most popular scriptures in the Bible used by Christian traditionalists in reference to homosexuality is the story of Sodom and Gomorrah as found in Genesis 19. Although there is much written on the topic, there are many things often missed about the story. Today, in our lesson, we will share some of this information in the hope of bringing a clearer picture of what actually took place there around 1900 B.C.

Background information

The city of Sodom is first mentioned in Genesis Chapter 13. Abraham and Lot (Abraham's nephew) set out to settle in new land. They came to realize that, between the two of them, they possessed so much that any area in which they were living could not hold the both of them. So they decided to separate.

Genesis 13 :11 11 Then Lot chose all the plain of Jordan; and Lot journeyed east: and they separated themselves the one from the other.

The area of Sodom and Gomorrah has been figured out by putting various descriptions in the Bible together. There has been much excavation there and satellite photos have confirmed the existence of ancient cities. At the time of this story, on the plains of Jordan which Lot chose, was a city called Sodom. Their people had already developed a fierce reputation long before what happened on the eve of their destruction. Six chapters before the event, in Genesis 13, it"s recorded that …..

Genesis 13: 13
….the men of Sodom were wicked and sinned before the Lord exceedingly.

The cities that occupied the land at this time were Sodom, Gomorrah, and three other cities, Admah, Reboiim, and Zoar. They were also known as Canaanites as they were descendants of Canaan who was a grandson of Noah. Noah is described in Genesis 6 saying …

Genesis 6:9
…..Noah was a just man and perfect, in his generations, and Noah walked with God.

However, the Canaanites culture had now descended into idol worship and we learn from later accounts that they hated outsiders and treated foreigners viciously and shamefully. There are a number of accounts in Jewish oral history that testify to their ungodliness. None of which speak to sexual offenses.

As the story continues in Genesis 14, we see a group of kings from the north banding together to invade and conquer the valley of Sodom and the other cities of the plain and they were successful. They looted the cities and took many captives into slavery, INCLUDING LOT. Abraham was informed of this and ......

Genesis 14:
14 ..... Armed his trained servants, born in his house, three hundred and eighteen, and pursued them into Dan.
15 And he divided himself against them, he and his servants by night, and smote them and pursued them unto Hoab, which is on the left hand of Damascus,
16 And he bought back all the goods, and also brought back his brother Lot, and his goods, and the women also, and the people.

Afterwards, the king of Sodom along with Melchizedek, king of Salem, met with Abraham to pay him tribute for his victory. The king of Salem offered him bread and wine. Abraham showed his appreciation by giving him a tenth of all that he owned. The king of Sodom then offered to Abraham all the loot he had recovered but Abraham (knowing Sodom's bad reputation) bluntly refused. He said .....

Genesis 14: 23
23 I will not take anything that is thine, lest thou shouldest say, I have made Abram rich;

The next mention of Sodom is in Genesis Chapter 18. Three messengers of God come to visit Abraham. While there, they contemplate whether they should share with Abraham a prophecy from the Lord regarding Sodom. They contemplated because they knew that Abraham had been promised by the Lord to be a great nation and yet his nephew's dwelling place was on the brink of destruction, as it says ......

Genesis 18: 20
20....Because the cry of Sodom and Gomorrah is great, and because their sin is grievous

Jewish tradition has it that visitors were mistrusted and taken hold of and robbed. They were left penniless in the streets and left to die. To care for them or feed them was against their laws.

Once again, we see Sodom's reputation preceding them. Abraham, when told of their impending doom, became distressed. He actually challenged God. He asked if He would destroy Sodom and Gomorrah if fifty righteous men could be found there. The Lord said He would spare them if there were fifty. Then Abraham, knowing the city's reputation, asked for mercy for the cities if there were only forty-five righteous. Again, the Lord said they would be spared if there were forty-five. From there, Abraham went to thirty to twenty and, finally, to as few as ten righteous. The Lord said they would be spared for ten. It should be noted that Sodom was very much backslidden LONG BEFORE the event that traditionalists say caused its downfall.

In Genesis 19, we find two of the messengers going to Lot's house in Sodom to determine if there were, indeed, any righteous among those in the city. When the people of the city learned that these outsiders had come to visit Lot, scripture says the mob …

Genesis 19: 4

4... compassed the house round, both old and young, ALL THE PEOPLE from every quarter.
5... And they called unto Lot and said unto him, "Where are the men that came in to thee this night? Bring them unto us that we may know them."

To calm the mob, Lot offered to send out his two virgin daughters. But the mob became indignant and ignored Lot's offer. They came near to breaking down the door (v. 9). At this point, the angels smote the men with blindness and said .....

Genesis 19: 13

13....We will destroy this place because the cry of them is waxen great before the Lord and the Lord has sent us to destroy it.

Scripture tells us that early the very next morning Lot, his wife and his two daughters left the city of Sodom and, upon their leaving, the cities were destroyed. The catastrophe forever changed the landscape around the Dead Sea area where the cities were located .

This area is located in the Middle East and sits atop a crack in the earth's crust. It's well known for its oil reserves. Sodom had a wealth of bitumen (brimstone). That's a sticky oily substance used for a multitude of purposes including home construction and for tarring roofs among other things. It is highly flammable.

The thinking is that an earthquake shifted the ground releasing natural gas that ignited from the hearth fires in homes. This resulted in massive explosions and destruction. With the earthquake, the Dead Sea broke through its southern border and flooded the valley of Sodom. Its destruction was complete.

Genesis 19: 24
***24**...the Lord rained upon Sodom and upon Gomorrah brimstone and fire from the Lord out if heaven.*

The View of Religious Traditionalist

The controversy about Genesis 19 revolves around the statement that the men of the city made to Lot that night about the visitors, Genesis 19: 5, "bring them out that we may *know* them". Religious tradition has taught us what the mystery behind why Sodom and Gomorrah were destroyed, lies behind the word "know". It is taught that this word reveals that the men were expressing a sexual desire to have homosexual relations with the visitors and, because of that, their cities were destroyed.

This belief is based on the original Hebrew word for the word "know", which is the word, "yada". It is the same word used in Genesis 4: 1 where it says............"Adam knew Eve his wife and she conceived and bore Cain". It is also used the same way regarding Cain and his wife as well as in Genesis 4: 25 and ten other references in the Bible.

Religious tradition teaches that the use of the word "know" in these references proves that the word "yada" means to "know one sexually" without compromise.

Therefore, if that definition holds for these references of the word "yada", it also holds for the Sodom reference as well. Therefore, according to their view, this proves the traditional belief that these men wanted to know these male angels in a sexual way.

Religious Traditionalists views are further supported by the belief that the men of Sodom rejected Lot's daughters that night because none of the men of Sodom had sexual desires for women but for men only. When they expressed this desire to "know" the angels instead, religious tradition says that this is when they were blinded. This further supports religious traditional views that "God will not tolerate homosexuality".

In reading these passages it's important to remember that the truths that scripture reveal will never be fully understood by anyone from mere reading or by shear meditation. It must be closely studied in its original languages and its verses, in their full contexts, for its greatest revelations.

The View According to the Original Written Word

Religious traditionalists are very correct in stating that the original Hebrew word for "know" is the word "yada". Where Religious traditionalists are not correct is in their definitions of and application of the word "yada". Although the word "yada" is, indeed, also found in the ten references mentioned above, the Hebrew word "yada" is also found 935 other places in scripture as well. However, in none of those places do traditionalists apply their same definition that they have applied to the Sodom story. It should be understood that the religious traditional definition, does not apply to every scripture and therefore should not be made to apply to Genesis 19.One of the places that the word "yada" is found in the Old Testament is in Genesis 45

Genesis 45: 1
45**.....*And there stood no man with him, while Joseph made himself* known *unto his brothers,* **46** *And he wept aloud: and the Egyptians and the house of Pharaoh heard*

The word "known" in this scripture also translates back to the Hebrew word "yada" in the same way that it translates back to it in the Adam and Eve story. If the traditionalists definition of the word "yada" is to be applied to every scripture, it would read this way: "And there stood no man with him, while Joseph made himself known sexually unto his brothers.

No one throughout the history of Judaism or Christianity has ever said that anything like that was suggested in this story. Why is it thought to be suggested in the Sodom story? In fact, no one suggested that the Sodom story was about sexual sin for 2,000 years. That notion was introduced by a Greek Jew named Philo who lived in the 1st century A.D., 2000 years after Sodom's destruction. One more example is ...

Isaiah 1: 3 3**.....*The ox* knoweth *his owner.*

Again, "knoweth" is "yada". No one has ever suggested that it is a bestiality passage. If "yada" under no certain terms, always

\

means "to know sexually", as I have heard many say, then why is it never applied here? The answer: Because , "to know sexually", is not the proper definition to the word.

Thank God for the Holy Spirit within and those who have made resources available to give us a clear understanding of languages !! According to the noted Robert E. Young, author of Young's Lexicon to the Old and New Testament, here is the proper translation of the Hebrew word "yada"............

YADA: *"To acquaint", "to familiarize"/ to come to understand. (Index Lexicon of the Old Testament)*

Nowhere in any lexicon that I have read, is the word "yada" ever translated to "know one sexually"---anywhere. Applying the PROPER TRANSLATION of "YADA" as opposed to the rather obscure traditional definition takes the mystery out of each story and gives the reader a much clearer idea of what is being said in every instance. When you apply the PROPER TRANSLATION to the Adam and Eve story, you know exactly without question what is meant when the word "yada" is used. According to scripture, Adam had never been with a woman before Eve.

When Adam became "familiar" with Eve, she conceived and bore Cain. Likewise, when Cain and his wife "familiarized" themselves to each other, she also conceived.

Young's translation also applies in the story of Joseph. Joseph's brothers had not seen him since he was a child so they had no idea what he looked like. It was when he made himself "yada"

to his brothers, and familiarized them with who he was, that
there was a great rejoicing in his family and the whole house
heard.

Correct Application:

Young's definition also applies in the Genesis 19 account of
Sodom. The two who came to the small city of Sodom were
extraordinary. The WORD calls them "angels".

Genesis 19: 1
*1....And there came two angels to Sodom, and Lot sat in the
gate of Sodom: And Lot, seeing them, rose up to meet them: and
he bowed himself with his face to the ground.*

To see an angel or any unfamiliar messenger there in Sodom,
was in no stretch of the word, typical. It only makes sense that
the people of Sodom , as vicious, possessive and evil hearted as
they were known to be, were upset when they heard that the
two unusual strangers had gotten into their town without their
knowledge . Who were these strangers? What are they doing
here? Have they brought something of value that we might
want? Can we take them down? We want to KNOW who they
are! Given Sodom's history, they had bad intent toward them.
Furthermore, Lot lived there. He knew how they treated
strangers who had gotten in and he feared for his guests.

The men of Sodom called out :

*(**paraphrased**) ...."Where are these men that have come to you
tonight? Send them out here that we may become familiar with
them."*

Upon hearing this demand, he responds, "Please don't be so wicked". And in a desperate attempt to side track them, he says "Behold I have two virgin daughters…"

Now, among the questions that come up in the Sodom controversy is, "Why were Lot's daughters *rejected* by heterosexual men? Religious traditionalist will say, because they were not heterosexual, but homosexual.

The truth to the matter is : They *rejected* the daughters because they were not there for sex at all (as suggested). They were there because they were angry about the men being in their city. The real question to religious traditionalist is : "If Lot knew he lived in a town full of homosexuals, then why did Lot agree to send his daughters out, instead of his sons-in law, who were also in the house as well(vs 12, 14). Nothing in the religious traditionalist's stories about this makes any sense .That's because it's a pack of lies.

What makes sense is : Lot knew that the majority of the men his town, like most towns, were heterosexual men and heterosexual men find women pleasurable, not men. That's why he agreed to send his daughters out, to appease and divert their attention. However, these men did not come to Lot's door because they were seeking sexual pleasure (as religious traditionalist say).There is nothing in scripture to suggest it. They were there to do what they typically always did whenever they learned strangers were in their town. They would take whatever valuables they had ,beat them and then throw outside of their city. Sodom was a rough gated community, one not welcoming to anyone coming in. They came as a mob that night to let Lot and all the men in the house know that they didn't like that these strangers had gotten in and they were there to throw them out.

The Bible says that (Genesis 19: 4) ...the men of the city, the men of Sodom, compassed the house round, both young and old, all the people from every quarter". All the people would include, the women and even the children! They were upset that Lot let these strange men into their town and they wanted to know "*and* become familiar with" who they were. It's only when you ADD the word SEX to this story, that it takes on the new meaning that tradition has added to it over the past few centuries. Some religious traditionalists have even changed the word "know" to "rape" in this passage where it would say "Send them out that we might *rape* them?" Yet the Hebrew word "yada" has nothing to with the word "rape" in its definition at all.

The whole male rape adage to the Sodom story is a total fabrication with no scriptural support for it anywhere else in the entire bible. That's another reason why it should be rejected. Remember, we use scripture to verify scripture.

Isaiah 28: 10
10**....**"*For precept must be upon precept .....line upon line*"

Despite whatever perceptions, possibilities and assumptions that can be invented about this verse, it is important that we understand that they are all just perceptions and possibilities and mere assumptions. What is important is that we understand what   IS clearly seen, without delving into mystery and assumed meanings because when we ADD to the scripture, confusion is introduced. In Revelation it says...

Revelation 22: 18

19...If any man shall add unto these things, God shall add unto him the plagues that are written in this book.

Nowhere does it say in scripture that Sodom was destroyed because the men of Sodom were homosexual. What the scripture does CLEARLY say about Sodom is ...*that (Gen. 13: 13) "the men of Sodom were wicked and sinners before the Lord exceedingly",(Gen. 8: 20) " ...their sin was grievous" and that (Gen. 9: 13) .."the cry of them was waxen before the Lord".* The suggestion that they were involved in homosexuality is nothing more than mere assumptions, opinions and speculation and is not based on the "Word".

To end all the speculation, however, THERE ARE SCRIPTURES WHERE THE PROPHETS TELL US EXACTLY WHAT SINS THE MEN AND WOMEN OF SODOM WERE GUILTY OF...........

Ezekiel 16: 49

49 Behold, this was the iniquity of thy sister Sodom, pride, fullness of bread, and an abundance of idleness was in her and in her daughters, neither did she strengthen the hand of the poor and needy. 50 And they were haughty and committed abomination before me: therefore I took them away as I saw good

Once again, we see scripture referring to the fallen state of those who lived during the days of Sodom and we see scripture mentioning the five major things that they were guilty of.

Not one of them suggests homosexuality, unless you ADD, speculate, invent and make assumptions.

2000 years later we find Sodom mentioned again in the scripture by a NEW Testament writer saying …

Jude 7….Sodom and Gomorrah and the cities about them in like manner, giving themselves over to fornication, and going after strange flesh, are set forth for an example, suffering the vengeance of eternal fire.

In this scripture, we see the reference that Sodom was guilty of fornication, which typically refers to sex outside of the bonds of a sacred marriage, a sin of which anyone can be guilty. The Greek word for the word "strange" is the word "heteros", which means " something other than their own", It is also the root word for "heterosexual".

Heterosexuals are attracted to a sex "other than" their own. Had the people of Sodom been guilty of going after "their own" kind, the writer would have used the Greek word "homo" flesh. The term used, however, is "heteros" meaning some flesh other than human flesh (such as animal flesh, as in bestiality). Again, nothing in this verse in Greek or English to suggest homosexuality but because it references Sodom, religious traditionalist apply it to gays to support their view.

One of the terms that the people of Sodom have become associated with in the past few centuries is the term "Sodomite". However, you will never find the people of Sodom referred to this way in the book of Genesis and, of course, after Genesis 19, their entire group had been wiped out.

Genesis 19: 24-25
24.....the Lord rained upon Sodom and Gomorrah brimstone and fire from the Lord out of heaven:
25 And he overthrew those cities, and all the plain, and all the inhabitants of the cities, and that which grew upon the ground.

The traditional belief is that whenever the word "Sodomite" is used in scripture, it refers to the people who lived in Sodom. However "Sodomites" are never referred to in the bible *until after all the people in Sodom were destroyed* . If all the people in Sodom were all destroyed that would have to mean Sodomites had to be people other than those who lived in Sodom. One scripture that mentions them was written hundreds of years later…

Deuteronomy 23: 17
17 There shall be no whore of the daughters of Israel nor a sodomite of the sons of Israel.

Most religious traditionalist believe when the word Sodomite is used in this verse or any verses that it is referring to homosexual. That's because they believe that all the men of Sodom were homosexual which we have already established wasn't true. What most religious traditionalists have not learned or shared is that the biblical terms "Sodom" and "sodomite" have no relation to each other at all.

Sodom is the actual Hebrew name that the city of Sodom bore. The term Sodomite is, however, an English term that religious traditionalists labeled gays thousands of years later, long after the bible was written.

In the bible the original Hebrew word written before being translated into English to Sodomite is the word "Qadesh". A "Qadesh" was a male involved in prostitution serving both male and female clients.

In the books of First and Second Kings, the Qadesh/Sodomites were found providing sexual services to reconcile people with idol gods and they did this right within the temple of Almighty God ! However, they were driven out, not because of homosexuality, but because of their worship of idol gods within the temple of God.

Although the Hebrew word "Qadesh" was later translated to the word "Sodomite", it should be understood that the "Qadesh/Sodomite" was never related to Sodom in any way. The city of Sodom was destroyed hundreds and hundreds of years before the "Qadesh/Sodomite" were ever recognized or spoken about.

Finally, in the same way that the term "Sodomite" was never written in the original Hebrew, it should be understood that the term "sodomy" is *never found in scripture*, either (not even in any of the latest versions---YET). It is a term that was developed around the 17th century, long after Sodom, long after the scripture was even written. It started as a name to dishonor the sexual acts of priests who broke their celibacy vows. Then, about 200 years later, when religious traditionalists began to say "homosexuality was the sin of Sodom" and that "sodomy" was then given to dishonor the sexual acts of those who were homosexual.

A Christian who allows his/her personal faith to be built on things just passed on by tradition and NOT SPOKEN by the Spirit of God is a person whose faith will continually be " tossed and driven with every wind of doctrine". A person, however, who allows his/her faith to be built on those things revealed to his/her spirit by the Living God, that are based on the original written word, is a person who's faith will never be shaken.

CHAPTER THREE
The Abomination and Curses of the Holy Law
A Study of Leviticus 18: 22 (Lev 20: 13)

Some of the least read books of the Bible by the overall Christian community are the books of the law (one in particular). It is least read because it contains tons of laws, abominations, penalties and curses that the overall majority believe do not apply to Christians today. We will center in on a couple of laws that religious traditionalists seem to insist be kept. That's because it appears to address an issue they have with those who are gay and lesbian. These laws are found in the book of the law called Leviticus in chapters 18 and 20.

BACKGROUND INFORMATION

The basis for all the biblical laws of God are found in the first five books of the Old Testament, which Jews, and many today call the Torah. These five books were written by Moses to be given to the children of Israel on instruction from the Lord, Himself.

Leviticus 1: 1,2
1 And the Lord called out to Moses and spake unto him out of the tabernacle of the congregation, saying, 2 Speak unto the children of Israel and say to them…

Written within these five books (The Torah) come 613 commandments which are called the Mitzvot ,commandments that Hebrews believe God spoke to Moses, written to be kept by ALL FAITHFUL JEWS.

In addition to the Mitzvot, there were also things believed by Hebrews to be inspired by God that were given to the prophets and rabbis, known as the Oral Torah. Both the Torah and books of the Oral Torah can be found today in what Christians call the Old Testament.

The Talmud, another writing esteemed highly among Jews, was written to *explain* and expand upon the Mitzvot. Each of these laws throughout the Torah can be broken down into six categories:

<u>Laws that pertain to:</u>
Agriculture
Festivals
Marriage
Tort laws Sacrifices and
Purity laws

If that's not enough, there is also a vast collection of teachings and rabbinical interpretations handed down over the centuries called the Midrashim. These have the force of the law for Jews as well.

Today, Jews are often criticized by traditional Christians for being too legalistic. To be fair, here is an explanation of their thinking by one Jewish scholar;

" *.....when properly observed, the legalistic aspect of traditional Judaism increases the spirituality in a person's life because it turns the most trivial, mundane acts into acts of religious significance......when you do these things (keep the laws) you are constantly reminded of your faith and it becomes* *an integrated part of your entire existence.*"

The book of Leviticus (found in the Torah) is one book of the law, which is often simply called THE book of the law. It was written by Moses in roughly a month's time (Exodus 40: 17 and Num 1:1) while the Hebrews were at Mt Sinai around 1445 B.C. These laws were given to the children of Israel (Hebrews/Jews) by the Lord who said unto them…..

Leviticus 20: 26
26 And ye shall be holy unto Me: for I the Lord am Holy and severed you (set you apart) from the other people, that ye should be mine.

Notice that these laws were to have a purpose: to keep the people holy and setting them apart from all pagan societies. These laws were important to keep because breaking the statutes meant breaking the covenant of God.

Leviticus 26: 15
15 And if ye shall despise my statutes or if your soul abhor my judgments, so that ye will not do all of my commandments, but that ye break my covenant
16 I will do this unto you; I will appoint over you terror, consumption, and the burning ague that consume the eyes and cause sorrow of heart: and ye shall sow seed in vain, for your enemies shall eat it.

The Lord also promised that if Israel would not keep His statutes they would be vomited out of the Promised Land (Lev 18: 24-30). Although some of the penalties for breaking those laws seemed to be uniquely severe, it is important to note that ALL ISRAEL could suffer from the transgressions of just a few. It is equally important to understand that each law was meant to be taken serious, so serious that two of Moses' own nephews were punished because they broke one sacrificial law.

Leviticus 10: 1,2
1 And Nadab and A-bi-hu, the sons of Aaron, took either of them his censer, and put fire therein, and put incense thereon, and offered strange fire before the Lord, which He commanded them not
2 And there went out a fire from the Lord, and devoured them, and they died before the Lord.

Although Jews and Christians alike view the Levitical laws as God's commandments, the Jews, as God's chosen people, view these commandments as being given to JEWS ONLY and NOT TO THE GENTILES. They maintain that Gentiles are only required to keep the 7 Noahide *statutes* based on things believed to be said by God to Noah in Genesis 9: 1-7. Most Jewish traditions believe these are the only laws given to ALL MANKIND.

The View of Religious Traditionalists

According to some Christians who are RELIGIOUS TRADITIONALISTS, however, the Levitical laws are still considered to be the laws of God for ALL PEOPLE. Many believe that those not committed to keep these laws of God (particularly the sexual laws) risk bringing the wrath of God upon everybody, the same as the Jews believe.

While many religious traditionalists esteem all the laws as laws of God, there are those who think some of the laws should be kept and people who say keeping others is no longer required . Among the laws that THEY SAY are to still required, is a law that they say "alone" clearly shows that God is against homosexuality. The law that THEY use to support this is found in Leviticus Chapter 18. It reads …

Leviticus 18: 22
22……..Thou shalt not lie with mankind, as with womankind: it is abomination.

If other scriptures are possibly vague or unclear, this one THEY say "when standing alone" proves their point without a shadow of a doubt. They go on to say that not only does it "alone" prove that all homosexual sex is unacceptable to God but that this scripture emphasizes that attitude by adding the ending statement that , "it is abomination" .

Remember: The truths scripture reveal, will never be fully understood by any from mere reading or by shear meditation. It must be closely studied in its original languages and its verses, in their full contexts, for its greatest revelations.

The View in the Original Written Word

Without a doubt, as religious traditionalists say, when Leviticus 18: 22 "stands alone", it does *appear* to show disapproval of homosexual sex. However, it is important to know that LEVITICUS 18:22 WAS NOT WRITTEN TO STAND ALONE and there are OTHER VERSES that lead in, follow and are connected to it.

Yet, when traditionalists quote it, it is always QUOTED alone without mentioning these other verses, thereby rendering only a "half truth" to the hearer. This leads a person to believe some things about Leviticus 18: 22 that ARE NOT ENTIRELY TRUE.

There are many scriptures in the Bible that are quoted exact to every word and that can be made to mean one thing when standing alone. But, when it is quoted IN PROPER CONTEXT, it will give an entirely different understanding. Here is one such example :

Deuteronomy 28: 28,29
***28** And the Lord will smite thee with madness and blindness and astonishment of heart:*
***29** And thou shall grope at noonday as the blind gropeth in darkness, and thou shalt not prosper in thy ways: and thou shalt only be oppressed and spoiled evermore, and no man shall save thee.*

Here we find two scripture verses that have been quoted entirely and EXACTLY THE WAY THEY ARE WRITTEN in the King James version of the Bible. They are also written in one in the books recognized as God's Holy Laws. If we believe that all of the bible is God speaking to all who serve Him, then, according to that belief, it's safe to say that it is written to us. If we take these verses as "stand alone", it tells us that God is going to drive us mad, make us blind cause us to stumble, fix it so we'll never prosper, always be oppressed and on top of all that, we won't be saved. Yet we say that we are all God's children, that God loves us all and would lead us out of bad situations. How can such a verse be written and believed, when we believe that the bible is all God's word and we're reading with our own eyes all the bad things He says He's going to do?

From reading that one scripture alone, one would never get that "God is good". Reading just that one scripture, one would actually see that God is EVIL! We see nothing here but an awful picture painted of Him and it's found right within the scriptures.

This is what may happen when scriptures are taken out of context. Other verses of scripture that go with it or are connected to it are not quoted with it. This happens all the time. Time and time again, people have taken scriptures (not just lay people but professors) and have used them and even written books to prove the "evil" nature of God.

However, what we must understand is that, even though THESE SCRIPTURES ARE WRITTEN IN THE BIBLE, they are not being read in the ORIGINAL CONTEXT in which they were written.

To be clear, if you read the very first line in that chapter, you will find out exactly who God is talking to and what He is talking about.

Deuteronomy 28: 1
1 And it shall come to pass if thou (whosoever is among you) shalt hearken diligently unto the voice of the Lord thy God to observe and to do all His commandments which I command thee this day, that the Lord thy God will set thee on high above all the nations of the Earth.

2 And all of these blessings shall come upon thee and overtake thee, if thou shalt hearken unto the voice of the Lord thy God.....

12 The Lord shall open upon thee His good treasure the heavens and give rain unto thy land in His season, and to bless all the work of thy hand, and thou shall lend unto many nations, and thou shalt not borrow

15 But it shall come to pass, if thou wilt not hearken unto the voice of the Lord thy God, to observe to do all His commandments and His statutes which I have commanded thee this day, that all these curses shall come upon thee and overtake thee.

28 The Lord shall smite thee with madness and blindness and astonishment of heart:

29 and thou shalt grope at noonday, as the blind gropeth in darkness, and thou shalt not prosper in thy ways: and thou shalt only be oppressed and spoiled evermore and no man shall save thee.

By reading the surrounding verses of these scriptures, one gains a MUCH CLEARER PICTURE of what Deuteronomy 28: 28, 29 is really talking about. The Lord does not curse those who love, *obey and keep His commandments*. God is a good God and, indeed, He promises only blessings to all those who OBEY Him. According to scripture, it was only those who choose to DISOBEY, that would find themselves going mad, blind, becoming poor and oppressed. It wasn't to come upon those who love Him and keep the commandments.

Those were things God said to the Jews who tracked and judged righteousness according to how the Mitzvot is kept. According to the Word of God, righteousness is no longer judged by the law.

Romans 3:21

21 But now the righteousness of God without the law is manifested, being witnessed by the law and the prophets.
22 Even the righteousness of God which is (now) by faith of Jesus Christ (is) unto all and UPON ALL THAT BELIEVE: for there is no difference

According to the New Testament writings, now all who believe in Jesus are seen by him as righteous , and because of that righteous standing, we need not "fear" the curses as …

Galatians 3: 13,14

13 Christ has redeemed us from the curse of the law, being made a curse for us: for it is written. "Cursed is every man that hangeth on a tree"
14 That the blessings of Abraham (which we read in Deut 28) might come on the gentiles through (their faith in) Jesus Christ.

Jesus knew the waywardness of mankind. He became cursed and took the punishment for all sin in place of those who would break His commandments but were committed to faith in Him, that they would have right standing in him. In doing this, those who are believers are redeemed from the curse that comes from breaking the law. According to New Testament scripture, the wage and curse due for breaking God's law, is death.

Romans 6:23

23 The wages of sin is (indeed) death: but the gift of God is eternal life through Jesus Christ our Lord

Those who believe on Jesus, because of his sacrifice, are no longer judged as righteous according to whether he keeps the law but whether he believes on Jesus. Those who believe are now seen by God as righteous, redeemed from the curse of eternal death, and now have eternal life based on what Jesus said in John 3:16.

The laws believers no longer have to keep to be judged as righteous also include the laws found in Leviticus 18. Let's look closer at these laws however, in their full context and original language, to see if they do apply to believers who are gay, as so many say today.

The very first verse of Leviticus 18 lets us know to whom these commandments of the law were directed:

Leviticus 18: 1-3
1 And the Lord spake unto Moses, saying, 2 Speak unto the children of Israel, and say unto them, I am the Lord your God.

This clearly tells us that these commandments set standards of righteousness for those who *were children of Israel* who had just been delivered from the idol worshipping culture of the Egyptians (about which we will speak later). These commandments or laws were not given to Christians, as the faith of Christianity had not been born until some 1500 years later. Once the Christian faith had come into existence, we are told by the founders of our faith that, Christians are under an entire new covenant.

Romans 3: 28

28 Therefore we conclude that a man (or woman) is (now simply) justified by faith (in Jesus) without (having to keep) the deeds of the law.

This NEW covenant is written about throughout the entire New Testament and most religious traditionalists who study the New Testament *know this*. All Christian religious leaders typically teach this concept in all churches when speaking of almost every law spoken about in Leviticus.

However, it is strange that the "justified by faith" concept, is almost always omitted, forgotten, never introduced or brought up by many Christians when it comes to homosexuality and a famous quoted scripture against it is Leviticus 18: 22 .

This is important to understand when it comes to religious traditionalists, that they are usually being unfair, because they generally all believe all Christians are justified by faith and are no longer under the laws in Leviticus. Nor do they hold their own selves to these laws. They will however, pull out the law mentioned in Leviticus 18:22 to a person who is gay, even though there is nothing in the law to justify their position which we will learn as we read further.

Before looking at Leviticus 18:22, to understand it clearly, it's important to read the entire passage that introduces it, as it's generally quoted out of context. In our study today we will read it in the context in which it was written and then look at the verse's original words. What you will see when read in its original language and context will be incredible and is much different than what's seen when quoted out of context.

Leviticus 18:3
3 After the doings of the land of Egypt, wherein ye dwelt, shall ye not do: and after the doings of the land of Canaan, whither I bring you ye shall not do: neither shall ye walk in their ordinances

In order to better understand some of the activities and ordinances that the people of Canaan were involved in, it would be helpful to look at another scripture. One such scripture that characterizes them throughout their story is ..

Exodus 23: 23,24
23 For mine angel shall go before thee, and bring thee unto the Amorites, and the Hittites, and the Perizzites, and the Canaanites, the Hivites, and the Jebusites: and I Will cut them off.
24 Thou shalt not bow down to their gods, nor shall serve them, nor do after their works: but thou shalt utterly destroy them, and quite break down their images.

We learned in our last lesson that the children of Israel were coming into the land of more Canaanites, who were the backslidden descendants of Noah. They also surrounded the area where the inhabitants of Sodom once lived. At this time all of the surrounding areas had fallen into idol worship which we know God detested more than anything. We know because the very first commandment He gave to Moses was…

Exodus 20: 3
3 Thou shalt have no other gods before Me.

As the writer of Leviticus continues in his laws in Chapter 18, we see the first laws that he addresses are 13 laws concerning ILLEGAL SEXUAL TEMPTATIONS involving people of kin. They begin with….

Leviticus 18: 6 *6 None of you shall approach to any that is kin to him to uncover their nakedness: I am the Lord.*

They continue for the next 14 verses mentioning those who are considered kin: father, mother, son, daughter, etc. The next verse (immediately after those 14) speaks of one law concerning ILLEGAL SEXUAL ACTS (none of which involve same sex relations).

Leviticus 18: 20
20 *Thou shalt not lie carnally with thy neighbor's wife, to defile thyself with her.*

It is important to note that IMMEDIATELY AFTER Moses mentions this one act and DIRECTLY BEFORE THE VERSE WE ARE CENTERING IN ON (22), we see entire new sets of sins beginning to be introduced in verse 21 which are ALMOST NEVER MENTIONED by those who quote verse 22.

This involves the RITUALISTIC SACRIFICES OF IDOL WORSHIPPERS performed to honor and bring pleasure to the idol god Molech. The first sacrifice which we find in the next verse is…

Leviticus 18: 21

21 And thou shalt not let any seed pass through the fire to Molech, neither shalt thou profane the name of thy God: I am the Lord.

Typically, when religious traditionalists quote the Leviticus 18: 22 scripture, they seem to always either conveniently, read fast through, ignore, skip and sometimes just TOTALLY OMIT this verse as if it means nothing and was just stuck in the middle of 20 and 22.

What we have discovered earlier from thoroughly reading all of the verses IN CONTEXT together is that this verse is not just stuck in the middle, but is directly connected to the verses that follow. Their connection, however, cannot become clear until one takes the time to find out WHO THIS GOD "MOLECH" was, why RITUALISTIC SACRIFICES to bring him pleasure are here, and how they are directly related to the other verses that follow.

Molech, who also had many other names, was a hollowed out image with the visage of a calf who was worshipped by the Ammonites, who ruled, at one time, over the land of Canaan. He is mentioned throughout the Old Testament and found in the New Testament as well. His name meant "King and god of the city", and according to the ordinances of "his" cities he was to be worshipped by all who entered the city in which he stood. This ordinance was also intended for the Israelites to obey, as well, as they had to pass through his city. However, the Lord had pre-warned them earlier in this chapter that…

Leviticus 18: 3
*3 ...after the doings of the land of Canaan, whither I bring you,
shall ye not do: neither shall ye walk in their ordinances.*

One of the ordinances from the Ammonites of Canaan was the
order to worship the god Molech in the ways he required.
Among those required was a list of ritualistic sacrifices that his
subjects were ordered to perform before him to pay homage and
to procure his favor and blessing. Beginning in Leviticus 18:
21, we find a list of 3 RITUALISTIC SACRIFICES
PERFORMED FOR THE GOD MOLECH, whom the Lord did
not want the children of Israel to do.

The FIRST RITUALISTIC SACRIFICE typically
PERFORMED FOR MOLECH"S PLEASURE that we see
Moses going into in verse 21, immediately AFTER mentioning
this ILLEGAL SEXUAL ACT, was the sacrifice of little
children…

Leviticus 18:21
*21 And thou shalt not let any of thy seed pass through the fire to
Molech, neither shalt thou profane the name of God: I am the
Lord*

Now, here it gets a little gruesome. The word "seed" in this
verse is a reference to children and the ritual, we are told,
involved bringing little children or babies to the huge golden
calf Molech and laying them on the palms of the idol's
outstretched hands. His hands were heated from the inside with
burning fire. The child lay there screaming until he/she passed
away as a result of the flames. It is important to note that
none of these sacrifices were designed to bring pleasure

to the participants but for the pleasure of Molech only. Jewish history tells us that as each of these sacrifices was performed for Molech and he or she who made the offering was to say "May it please YOU ! May it benefit YOU ! May it agree with YOU, OH Molech ! (see Deut 12: 31, II Kings 23: 10 and Jer 32: 35).

Another ritualistic sacrifice performed for Molech is listed RIGHT AFTER the verse which THIS LESSON is centered around in ….

Leviticus 18: 23
23 Neither shalt thou lie with any beast to defile thyself therewith; neither shall any woman stand before a beast to lie down thereto: it is confusion.

History tells us that these types of RITUALISTIC SACRIFICES were among many TYPICAL SACRIFICES PERFORMED BEFORE IDOLS of that day, such as before Baal, which guaranteed fertility to the worshiper (or his animals or his crops). Again, however, as with all sacrifices to idols, they were performed as serious sacrifices to bring PLEASURE TO THAT IDOL for his blessings. They were not ordered by the priests as a means of allowing those who approached to have sexual pleasure. A sacrifice such as that would be judged as insincere.

The verse about which THIS LESSON is centered is found within this SAME LIST of RITUALISTIC SACRIFICES typically performed before Molech to bring him pleasure.

It is ..
Leviticus 18: 22
22 *Thou shalt not lie with mankind, as with womankind, it is an abomination.*

Many of the idols of that day were known for many things. History tells us that Molech was often called the god of fire. It also tells us that he is remembered as a god that promised fertility. We are told that a person who was not fertile was oftentimes REQUIRED, and even forced to go before a priest of the idol (which we learned from our last lesson was a qadesh) who stood before the huge idol wearing a large calves mask.

There, this subject would be required to have sex with the priest wearing the mask. He, in turn, would guarantee the subject's fertility. One such scripture where similar types of intimacy with idols is commanded of its idol worshipers, is found in Hosea 13: 2.

Another thing that should be remembered as we look at these RITUALISTIC SACRIFICES mentioned in Leviticus 18: 20-23 is that these acts, as with the other sacrifices mentioned, were not done in private as most intimate sexual acts are done. These acts were done publicly before the idol, his priest and subjects to bring that *idol* pleasure, as the worshiper said "May it please YOU! May it benefit YOU! May it agree with YOU, Oh Molech!

What we find particularly interesting about the Leviticus 18: 22 scripture is that, it is NOT LISTED with the list of ILLEGAL SEXUAL TEMPTATIONS AND SEXUAL OFFENSES. It IS listed however, WITH the list of RITUALISTIC SACRIFICES to Molech, as it is the worship of Molech which God detests. The sexual offenses God warned against are found in verses 6-20 of Leviticus 18 and nowhere in those verses is any mention of same-gender sex. Had same-gender sex been the issue, Moses would have included it right along with the group of sexual offenses mentioned and would have also included the mention of same-gender sex AMONG FEMALES as well but neither are found mentioned in his list.

The greatest support for this concept, however, comes from looking at the word "womankind". AS IT IS WRITTEN IN THE SCRIPTURE IN ITS ORIGINAL HEBREW. The Hebrew word written where the word "womankind" appears in this scripture is the word „ISHSHAH".

What we find from "Strong's Online Concordance" about "ISHSHAH" is that it is ONLY FOUND TRANSLATED BY THE TRANSLATORS ONE TIME in the entire Bible as the word "womankind", but found translated 78 times to the word "SACRIFICE and OFFERING". One of the places we find the word "ISHSHAH" mentioned is ..

Numbers 29: 36
36 But ye shall offer a burnt offering, a sacrifice made by fire

The word found where the phrase "sacrifice made by fire" is used, is the Hebrew word "ISHSHAH". It is the exact same word found in Leviticus 18: 22 for "womankind" spelled the exact same way according to Strong's Concordance and ALL ENGLISH TRANSLATORS. It is also written the exact same way in ancient Hebrew.

However, it is only in Leviticus 18: 22 that it seems the King James translators found it necessary to change the word „ISHSHAH" to "womankind" instead of the way it is translated in the other 78 verses. (The ancient Hebrew word for "woman" found in "Strong's Online" is the word "nashim").

An offering made by fire   [801] אִשֶּׁה ishshah

A sacrifice made by fire   [801] אִשֶּׁה ishshah

Womankind   [802] אִשֶּׁה ishshah

Strong"s also tells us that the ancient Hebrew word for the word "with" here is "im" and is often translated as the word "like". It is when we understand THE ORIGINAL CONTEXT in which Leviticus 18: 22 was written and these two more fitting translations of the words :im" and "ishshah", that we come to understand the issues that Moses addresses.

Thou shalt not lie with mankind AS - LIKE - A - (ritualistic) SACRIFICE. It is an abomination.

In the Leviticus 20: 13 verse, we find the word "ishshah" mentioned again and again and not "nashim". This time mentioning a "penalty" of those who sleep with other men "as a sacrifice". Here again in verses prior you will find references to Moloch and the penalty for Israel participating in this sacrifice was death, and it was spoken to be taken seriously.

Much later, however, we find the Lord putting a halt to many of the laws that He had put in place because of the insincerity that seemed to surface among those who "claimed" to abide by it. One such law that He no longer desired, was the law requirement to bring burnt sacrifices to be offered up.

Isaiah 1: 11-13

11 What to Me is the multitude of your sacrifices? Says the Lord: I have had enough of burnt offerings of rams and the fat of the fed beast. I no longer delight in the blood of bulls or of lambs or of goats.

12 When you come to appear before Me, who asked this from your hand? Trample My courts no more:

13 bringing offerings is futile; incense is an abomination to Me. New moon and Sabbath and calling of convocation---I cannot endure solemn assemblies with iniquity.

So it's obvious that many of the laws that God once required of Israel, he later discontinued (as in the sacrificial laws we just read in Isaiah). Then, in Jeremiah 31: 31, we find mentioned an entire new covenant of laws being introduced by the Lord. In that covenant, He said that He would place the laws on the inside of individual hearts of those who would believe on His son whom He would send. Then, the Son that He promised came through the person of Jesus Christ. According to scriptures, once we receive His Spirit into our hearts, we then become His children and heirs to ALL of the "precious promises" in His Word as we yield to His laws which He now confirms from "within our hearts".

CHAPTER FOUR

Paul's "Affections"
and the "Effeminate"
in the Ancient Greek Letters

A study of Romans 1, II Corinthians 6,
I Timothy 1 and II Timothy 3

Paul, the Apostle most responsible for the establishment of the church of Jesus Christ, lived during the Roman and Greek era. Many "religious traditionalists" say his writings express nothing but God's contempt for all homosexuals. Many who have looked closer at Paul's writings, however, say differently.

Today we will take a closer look at Paul and some New Testament passages that "religious traditionalists" use to support their views about in Romans 1: 26-28, II Corinthians 6 , I Timothy 1, and II Timothy 3: 2. To come to a good accurate conclusion, we will give a little history and look at these verses in their original context. We will also study their words in their original languages to see if the view that "religious traditionalists" hold is, indeed, supported by scripture.

Background Information

One of the most important and influential Apostles of Christianity was Paul of Tarsus (originally Saul) who, although he lived during Jesus's lifetime, never met Jesus during His ministry. Paul was born at Tarsus in Asia Minor (modern Turkey) in 10 A.D. By birth, he was officially a Roman citizen. He was raised in a culture heavily influenced by Greece and spoke Greek fluently. Before becoming a Christian he was a member of the Pharisees. As we shared in an earlier lesson, this religious organization highly honored the Oral Torah and very strictly adhered to its laws. We also shared how the Oral Torah was different than the Torah. It not only contained the words God said to Moses but the words inspired by God given to Prophets and Rabbis, as well. From his writings we can tell that he was not just a Pharisee but a very devout one. He says in ....

Philippians 3: 5

5 (I was) circumcised the eighth day of the stock of Israel, (I was) of the tribe of Benjamin, a Hebrew of Hebrews: as touching (or concerning) the law, a Pharisee.
6 Concerning zeal, persecuting the church, touching the righteousness which is in the law, blameless.

As mentioned, Paul spent much of his early life persecuting Christians who he considered to be heretics to Judaism. That all changed, however, when Paul beheld the risen Christ on the road to Damascus.

Acts 26: 13

13 At midday, O king, I saw in the way a light from heaven, above the brightness of the sun, shining round about me and them which journeyed with me. 14 And when we were all fallen to the earth, I heard a voice speaking unto me and saying in the Hebrew tongue, Saul, Saul why persecutest thou Me? It is hard for thee to kick against the pricks.

15 And I said "Who art thou Lord? And He said "I am Jesus whom thou persecutest.
16 But rise and stand upon thy feet: for I have appeared unto thee for this purpose, to make thee a minister and a witness...
18 To open their eyes and to turn them from darkness to light, and from the power of Satan unto God, that they may receive forgiveness of sins, and inheritance among them which are sanctified by faith that is in Me. (also see Acts 9: 1-20)

Being personally chosen by Jesus Christ to spread the Gospel, Paul pursued his new career with the same zeal he had for persecuting Christians and was instrumental in establishing churches throughout the land.

His main debate with the other Jewish Christian converts in his letter to the Romans was with the Old Testament Jewish laws and whether they were essential to justification for eternal life. His argument was that the law was useless in that respect and that the sacrifice of Christ and the faith acceptance of Jesus as Lord, was enough.

Romans 3: 28
28Therefore, we conclude that man (or woman) is justified by faith without having to keep the deeds of the (Old Testament) law... ....

It should be noted that when Paul spoke of the message he preached, he said ....

Galatians 1: 12
12 For I neither received it (his message) of man, neither was I taught it, but by the revelation of Jesus Christ.

Paul's conviction and strong message of justification through faith in Jesus Christ, confirmed by the many miracles he wrought, allowed Christianity to spread rapidly throughout the non-Jewish (gentile) population. He was so effective in proclaiming the Gospel that most of the New Testament, that Christians adhere to, is made up, in large part, of all the letters he wrote expressing his faith.

His letter, along with the Gospels and all of the letters written by the other Apostles, have been accepted by Christians as divinely inspired by God for the Church. Having been the founding blocks of Christianity since its inception, these letters have also been accepted as scripture for the church today in the same way that the laws of Moses were accepted as the Word of God to those of the Jewish faith, thereby carrying the same authority.

II Timothy 3: 16,17
***16** All scripture is given by inspiration of God, and is profitable for doctrine, for reproof, for correction, for instruction in righteousness*
***17** That (every) man (and woman) of God may be perfect, (and) thoroughly furnished unto all good works.*

The View of Religious Traditionalist

Although Paul's letters have, indeed, become the written Word of God for the church today, it should be noted that his letters did not gain that authority without controversy. In the same ways that many of the Hebrews disagreed and rebelled against the things that Moses set forth in his day, many Christians, in his time, also disagreed and rebelled against the things Paul set forth and continue to do so to this day.

Many "religious traditionalists", say that the people most rebellious of our day against Paul's teachings are those who are gay and lesbian. "Religious Traditionalists" hold this view because they say those who are gay, continue to engage in activity that they believe Paul says in scripture, that the Lord is against. One of the scriptures they use to support this is found in his letter to the Romans 1: 26,27. (

NOTE: Typically, when the subject of homosexuality and the scripture is discussed, Leviticus 18: 22 is the scripture referred to (see section on abominations). Many know, however, that the Leviticus scripture is just one of many Old Testament laws that the New Testament Christian no longer has to adhere to (read above in Romans 3: 28). The Leviticus scripture is particularly not as effective when it is used against those who are lesbian because its English versions says absolutely nothing about women and only refers to men. The scripture referred to in Romans is different in its English version. It is NOT in the Old Testament but IS in the New Testament and its English version DOES speak to women and thereby *"appears"* to be more effective in supporting the religious traditional view against gays. It reads…

Romans 1: 26, 27
26 For this cause, God gave them up unto vile affections: for even their women did change the natural use into that which is against nature:
27 Likewise also the men leaving the natural use of the women, burned in their lust one toward another: men with men working that which was unseemly, and receiving in themselves the recompense of their error which was meet.

As stated many times throughout this book , the truths that scripture reveals, will never be fully understood by anyone from mere reading or by shear meditation. It must be closely studied in its original languages and its verses in their full contexts, for its greatest revelations

. *The View in the Original Written Word*

When reading or hearing this scripture ALONE, which "religious traditionalists" use to support their anti-gay view, it is very easy to see why someone would believe God is against ALL people who are gay and lesbian. It is particularly convincing when someone tells you before the scripture is even quoted, that the "them" God is referring to are all homosexuals.

Romans 1: 26a
26 For this cause God gave THEM up to vile affections..

If a person who hears this has also been taught that homosexuality is against nature, when the end part of verse 26 is added, then that belief seems to be even further confirmed.

Romans 1:26b
26....for even their women did change the natural use into that which is AGAINST NATURE.

However, there's nothing in that scripture that says God gave all homosexuals up into vile affections and there is no need to read that into it. The scripture is very clear to us who God gave up to vile affections. To see this, however, one must read them in the context in which they were written and look at the other verses prior to gain clarity.

Who WAS Paul referring to when he said "them" ? The clue becomes clear when backing up to verse 18, where Paul begins explaining "who" the "them" was.

Romans 1: 18
18 For the wrath of God is revealed in heaven against all ungodliness and unrighteousness of MEN WHO HOLD THE TRUTH IN UNRIGHTEOUSNESS.

These are the people who God gave up unto "vile affections" (defined later). The original Greek word "hold" is the word "katecho" which means " to hold or keep back". This lets us know that he is referring to those working who keep "the truth" from going forth.

John 14: 6
6 Jesus said I am the way, the truth, and the life: no man cometh unto the Father but by Me.

This message of Jesus had just begun to be preached throughout the world that God had given to His people to declare. They preached the truth about Jesus, who He was, that He was the Son of God, that through His shed blood, there was remission of sin and that after His death He rose again.

Yet, many had united themselves together to keep that message from going forth. Paul, himself after becoming born again, disassociated from the Pharisee's, who were united to keep that truth from going forth. Those are the people he said "the wrath of God was against" . He's spoke against *them* because they had united themselves to hold back the work that Jesus had commissioned His followers to go forth in.

Mark 16: 15
16 Go ye into all the world and preach the gospel TO EVERY
CREATURE.

To those who worked to stop this, Paul says that it is the „wrath
of God" that is against "them". While it's true that there may be
many who are working today to STOP the preaching of the
gospel in our world, it should be noted that there are thousands
of born again, spirit-filled believers in the gay community *who
have dedicated their lives* to getting the gospel out. And Gods
wrath in no way is against that.

For God to pour out His wrath against anyone committing their
lives to Jesus and to getting His gospel out would prove to be
counterproductive to His own "great commission". Those who
state He hates followers contradict "the Word".

Romans 10: 15b
*15.... How beautiful are the feet of them that preach the gospel
of peace ...*

God's wrath is against those who *reject* the gospel. Those
committed to it are saved from His wrath.

Romans 5:9
*11 Much more than being justified by his blood, we shall be
saved from the wrath through Him.*

Verse 21 of Romans gives an even more distinct description of
those Paul spoke against. In this description, he spoke of those
who....

Romans 1: 21
21…. Knew God and glorified Him not as God, neither were thankful……

Again, this lets us know that Paul is not referring to persons who have dedicated their lives to God, but to persons not dedicated to God. Those persons who have purposed in their hearts to glorify God, give Him praise and remain thankful unto Him are not among the group His wrath is against. It is those who do not glorify him and are not thankful that he speaks against , according to what written in this verse.

Then in verse 23, Paul tells us exactly what these persons were doing that confirmed that they had no honor for God in their lives. He shows us that they had no commitment to worship God, at all. They were worshipping idols. He said that they were changing the glory of the incorruptible God. They worshiped gods who were ..,

Romans 1: 23
23… into an image made like a corruptible man, and to birds, and to four legged beasts and creeping things

Forbidding the worship of idols is not some unknown command in the Holy Law. One doesn't need to read through hundreds of laws before they find it. The command that these people were breaking was, indeed, the very first of the Ten Commandments penned by God himself. The first Commandment reads …

Exodus 20: 3
3 Thou shalt have no other gods before Me.

Yes, it does matter what God you worship. The God of Israel commands that *His* people worship Him and Him only and according to the Word, those who worship other gods have the wrath of God against them. Those of us, however, who have submitted to Him by making His Son Jesus the Lord of our lives have…

I Thessalonians 1: 9,10
9…..*turned to God FROM IDOLS to serve the true and living God*
10..*to wait for His Son from heaven, whom He raised from the dead, even Jesus who (has)* **delivered us from the wrath to come.**

According to the Word, all those **whose faith lie in Jesus**, men, women, old, young, good, bad, rich, poor, gay, and straight , shall be delivered from any wrath to come for the Word says…

John 3: 16 16….*that whosoever believeth in Him shall not perish, but have everlasting life.*

The believer has been washed in the blood and has thereby been made righteous by the blood. The unbeliever, however, has not been washed and therefore is named among the unrighteous because he has refused to believe on Jesus . Of them, the unrighteous, he says in…

I Cor 6: 9
9 *Know ye not the unrighteous shall not inherit the kingdom of God? Be not deceived, neither fornicators, nor idolaters, nor adulterers, nor effeminate, or abusers of themselves with mankind ……..shall inherit the kingdom of God.*

This passage above is another famous scripture in the New Testament that "religious traditionalists" often use along with Romans 1: 26 to show God's disdain for homosexuals, mainly because of the word "effeminate". However, looking at the word "effeminate" and its definition as it was originally written in the Greek, one finds an entirely different meaning.

The original Greek word where the word "effeminate" appears, is the word "malakos" and nowhere in its definition is there any mention of the word "feminine", or "male who is feminine acting or practicing" as we know the word today. Its definition is "one who is weak or weak in faith" .The Tyndale Bible, as we read in the introduction (written many years before King James) was the very first bible translated directly from the Greek to English. It is in this early bible that we find this scripture as it originally appears.

I Cor: 6: 9 Tyndale
9 Be not deceived, neither fornicators, neither worshippers of images, neither whoremongers, neither the weak.....shall inherit the Kingdom of God.

Christians are *commanded* throughout scripture to be "Strong in the Lord" (Ephesians 6:10). It's those who are strong in the Lord that will inherit the Kingdom of God, not those who are weak. So once again we find a scripture that never originally applied to gays that Religious Traditionalists have targeted.

The 2nd phrase *"abusers of themselves with mankind"*
is also found in I Timothy 1: 10. The Greek word for the phrase is the word " arsenokoites " which is only found in the

bible in these two verse's. Actually, it is not found anywhere else in all of Greek literature. According to Strong's Concordance reference 733, it refers to the Hebrew term "qadesh".

We learned in previous chapters that "the qadesh" was a male priest of an idol god (and qadisha was the female priestess) who required sex from their worshippers (both male and female) before their idol could grant them the blessings they desired be it children, rain for crops, etc. (see section on the Abomination) At any rate, we find it is the person involved in idol worship and not to the gay born-again believer, that is denied the blessings   of   God's   kingdom.

Paul says that it was these people who rejected the gospel of Christ that God gave over to "vile affections" so they could continue to do these ungodly forms of idol worship. Paul said…

Romans 1: 26
26…even their women did change the natural use into that which was against nature
27 And likewise the men also… …...

Traditionally, this scripture is used to point out that homosexuality is "unnatural and therefore against God". However, as in other scriptures, it is just as necessary to take into account the surrounding scriptures and how they were written in the original Greek words.

To keep this context, let us remember that it is the men and women involved in "idol worship" that are being referred to and YES when King James version says that they were doing things against nature he WAS referring to sexual practices among people of the same gender.

However, (just as in I Cor. 6: 9) the King James version fails to express Paul's original perceptions that he wrote in Greek. The word that appears in the original Greek for "nature" or "against nature" can be found in any exhaustive Bible concordance. It is the word "phusis" and means "common".

This helps to describe exactly what was going on among those involved in this "idol worship". They were going "against" all of the common practices God ordained for His worship. These were not people who loved God in any sense or had any allegiance to Him. They were people who had consciously left God to serve "idol images".

Romans 1: 21
21...(Those who) knew God and glorified Him not as God, neither were thankful...

These people had left God totally to worship idols and their uncommon practices of worship (which involved sex) eventually led them into VERY UNCOMMON SEXUAL PRACTICES with each other.

Romans 1: 27
27...and the women BURNED in their lust one towards another, (as did the) men with men.

The Greek word for "lust" in this passage is "orexis" which refers to an "over excessive" sexual drive.

It is important to note here that it was not the "homosexual relationships" themselves that were so uncommon among the people of this ancient Roman and Greek era. Actually, homosexuality in these countries was very, very common. What WAS uncommon, particularly to believers, during this era, was the sexual worship customs of these "fanatical idol worshippers" which often REQUIRED believers to have sex with priests, beasts and often each other.

The Lord has always spoken over and over again throughout the history of the bible to his people about submitting to idol worship. He's done it in much more than in just 7 scripture verses. There are actually more than 200 scriptures in the Word that warn against idol worship which is what Paul referred to in this chapter. He is merely affirming all the previous warnings spoken against it beforehand. God detests it.

Leviticus 19: 4
4 TURN YE NOT unto idols, nor make to yourselves molten gods.

That said, it should be noted again here, homosexual relationships themselves, were very common. This was very well documented in history at that time, going back as far as 300 years before Christ. It had become even more accepted by Rome during the time that Paul wrote this letter to the Romans. What we are reading was written in the first century. History gives well known accounts of same gender love has being common in ancient days as far back the 3rd century BC, which includes Alexander the Great, his father Philip, Julius Caesar. All very famous men and all known to have male lovers.

As far as women, there is much information about documented of their same gender love relationships as well, including the great female poet Sappho from those days who lived on the isle of Lesbos. There was also Augustus who lived during Jesus time. When Paul was actually writing to the Romans, Nero was emperor. The emperor Nero not only was known to have male lovers, he officially married his partner Sporus. It probably was the very first documented same-sex marriage ever. Also keep in mind that popular leaders have almost always been known for setting the trends for the more common folks, even as they do today. What happened among the more common folk however, were almost never documented, as the cases were among the influential.

So Paul, in his letter to the Romans, would have never written that it was the same sex relationships that were "uncommon" (as we shared earlier is the correct Greek translation for the word unnatural) .It was the idolatry that was uncommon among believers. Truth is, based on all the many erotic statues and pictures and books we have today from that time, same sex relationships were probably just as popular, if not more, in the Greek and Roman- Greek Era, than they are today. The well respected book written by Polybius, dating back to ancient Rome states, "MOST young men of that country had male lovers".

History further lets us know that same gender love was so common that they were referred to by very common terms known in that day, the same way we use the term "gay". The passive partner in a male relationship was known as the "caenide" (cain-a dee). The aggressive partner in a male relationship was known as " exoleti" (ex-o-leet-tee). Older men involved in steady relationships with younger men were referred to as "phillerastes" (philler-as-tees) and the younger man involved was referred to as "pederastes (ped-er-as-tees) and the list goes on.

It would seem that, as popular as homosexuality was during this time and as "detestable" as "religious traditionalists" say God was toward those in this lifestyle, it would seem that the terms commonly used *would appear somewhere in the original scriptures denouncing them*, **but they are found nowhere**. The Old Testament never speaks against it, Jesus never spoke against it and neither does Paul speak against them in these verses..only against those who were idol worshippers. Paul goes on to say…….

Romans 1: 28-31
28 (These idol worshippers) did not (even) like to retain God in their knowledge, (so) God gave them over to a reprobate mind to do things which were not convenient.
29 Being filled with unrighteousness, fornication, wickedness………
30 Backbiters, haters of God…………
31 Without understanding, covenant breakers, without natural affection

The Greek term used where "unnatural affections" appears is also seen in verse 26 in Romans, in Colossians 3:5 (rendered "inordinate affection") and in II Timothy 3: 3.

II Timothy 3: 2-3
2 For men shall become lovers of their own selves covetous, boasters, proud blasphemers, disobedient to parents, unthankful, unholy,
3 Without natural affection.

This scripture was covered in much detail in Chapter 1. The Greek word for the word "without natural affection" is the word "astergo". It is taken from the root word "stergo" which is one of the many Greek words for "love". There is "agape" which is the "love of God", "eros" which is "sexual love", "phileo" which is "brotherly love" and "stergo"(our word) which is the love of family or nation.

The word "**A**stergo" is the absence of the " love of family or nation". First translated by William Tyndale from Greek to English as one unkind, *unloving as one unloving unto his family or nation.* Those who have no love for family, are those who have totally forsaken the love of God and Paul says in the Romans 1, the chapter of our focus, that it is they that are "worthy of death" (Rom 1: 32), not those who are gay.

Thank God that those who believe on Jesus and trust in His blood are not included among those condemned.

I Cor 6: 11
11...but YE are washed, Ye are sanctified, but Ye are justified in the name of the Lord Jesus, and by the Spirit of our God.

Romans 6: 1-2, 22
1 What shall we say then? Shall we continue in sin that grace may abound?
2 God forbid........
22 But now being made free unto sin, and become servants unto God, ye (now) have your fruit unto holiness, and the end everlasting life.

Being washed, forgiven, and having a seat reserved in Heaven does not give one license to have sex with whatever, whoever and whenever we want. According to the Word, sex belongs in a marriage bed and in the bonds of a contracted marriage. That is the standard of holiness that we should seek to honor and uphold. It applies to all believers, heterosexual as well as homosexual.

Hebrews 13: 4
Marriage is honorable IN ALL and the (marriage) bed undefiled.